AF413515

# INDIA ON THEIR SHOULDERS

## LIVES THAT INSPIRE CONTINENTS

DR. MINAKSHI BANSAL

# DEDICATION

*This book is dedicated to the spirited people of India, whose resilience, wisdom, and enduring pursuit of progress continue to inspire the world. May the stories within these pages serve as a tribute to every unsung hero and every quiet struggle that has contributed to shaping a nation rich in diversity and strength. Let us all draw inspiration from these lives to foster a future replete with innovation, harmony, and enduring hope.*

# Contents

# Contents

# Prayer

*"Om Bhadram Karnebhih Shrinuyama Devah*
*Bhadram Pashyemakshabhiryajatrah*
*Sthirairangais Tushtuvamsastanubhih*
*Vyashema Devahitam Yadayuh*
*Svasti Na Indro Vriddhashravah*
*Svasti Nah Pusha Vishwavedah*
*Svasti Nastarkshyo Arishtanemih*
*Svasti No Brihaspatir Dadhatu*
*Om Shantih Shantih Shantih"*

*This mantra is a prayer for universal well-being, invoking the blessings of various deities for protection, health, and happiness. It emphasizes the importance of experiencing the auspicious through all senses and living a life aligned with divine purpose. The repetition of "Shantih" at the end signifies a deep desire for peace in the individual, the environment, and the universe at large. This mantra is often recited as a prayer for peace, prosperity, and the physical and spiritual well-being of all beings.*

ॐॐॐ

# About The Author

Dr. Minakshi Bansal, born in the bustling metropolis of Delhi, India, has led a life steeped in artistry, scholarly pursuit, and an unwavering commitment to societal betterment. Following her marriage, she relocated to Ahmedabad, Gujarat, where she has since blossomed into a multifaceted beacon of inspiration for many. Dr. Minakshi is not only recognized as a gifted artist in the realm of Fine Arts but also as an esteemed author, a devoted social worker and a dedicated research scholar in Psychology. Her journey, marked by a profound dedication to elevating those around her, especially the downtrodden and underprivileged children of society, is a testament to her deep-seated belief in the transformative power of engagement and empathy.

From her earliest days, Minakshi was distinguished by an insatiable appetite for reading. Her literary universe was inhabited by characters and narratives that spanned ethical tales, motivational and inspirational stories, and the mythic parables imbued with life lessons. This voracious reading habit was not merely for personal edification but was driven by a desire to distill and disseminate the essence of these narratives to foster the development of students and peers alike. She was particularly captivated by the lives and teachings of historical figures and spiritual leaders such as Adi Shankaracharya, Swami Vivekananda, Dr. APJ Abdul Kalam, Mahamana Pandit Madan Mohan Malviya, Mahatma Gandhi, Sardar Vallabhai Patel, and Vinoba Bhave, among others. Their philosophies and life stories fueled her ambition to embody their ideals of resilience, selflessness, and relentless pursuit of knowledge.

Dr. Minakshi's academic and practical engagement with psychology has been equally noteworthy. As a research scholar, her focus has been on exploring the intricate tapestry of the human psyche, aiming to unlock the potential for psychological well-being and societal harmony. Her scholarly work is complemented by her active involvement in social work, where she employs her academic insights to make tangible differences in the lives of the underprivileged. Her endeavours in social work are characterized by an innovative approach that combines traditional wisdom with contemporary psychological practices to address the multifaceted challenges faced by these communities.

Her artistic talents, another facet of her diverse capabilities, are not merely a personal passion but also serve as a medium through which she communicates and connects with others. Her art, rich in symbolism and emotional depth, reflects her philosophical inquiries and social concerns, offering viewers a glimpse into the breadth of her intellect and the depth of her compassion.

In addition to her contributions to the arts and social sciences, Dr. Minakshi has embraced the healing arts of Pranic Healing, mastering the techniques developed by Master Choa Kok Sui. This practice, which focuses on the manipulation of Prana or life energy to heal the body and aura, has been both a personal journey of discovery and a means through which she extends her healing touch to others. Her proficiency in Pranic Healing is complemented by her advocacy and teaching of various forms of meditation aimed at rejuvenation, personal betterment, and the cultivation of harmony within individuals and communities alike.

Dr. Minakshi's life is a narrative of relentless pursuit, not just of personal achievement but of the upliftment and empowerment of society at large. Her diverse interests and talents—spanning the arts, literature, psychology, and the healing practices—converge on a singular path of service. She embodies the spirit of the luminaries who inspired her, channelling their legacy through her actions and teachings. Through her books, art, and social initiatives, she continues to inspire a new generation to embark on their own journeys of self-discovery, resilience, and altruism.

Her commitment to social betterment, particularly her focus on uplifting underprivileged children, reflects a deep understanding of the transformative potential of education and personal development. By integrating her knowledge of psychology, her artistic sensibilities, and her healing practices, Dr. Bansal has developed a holistic approach to social work that addresses both the immediate needs and the long-term well-being of the communities she serves.

As an author, Dr. Minakshi's writings offer a blend of inspirational insights, practical wisdom, and reflective contemplations drawn from her extensive reading and life experiences. Her books serve as a guide for those seeking to navigate the complexities of life with grace, resilience, and purpose. Through her narratives, she extends an invitation to her readers to explore the depths of their own potential and to contribute meaningfully to the collective well-being of society.

In Dr. Minakshi Bansal, we find a remarkable synthesis of the artist, the scholar, the healer, and the social activist. Her life's work stands as a beacon of hope and a source of inspiration for individuals seeking to make a difference in the world. Her story is a compelling reminder of the power of individual action, rooted in compassion and driven by a profound commitment to the betterment of humanity. Dr. Minakshi's legacy is not just in the tangible outcomes of her efforts but in the enduring spirit of inquiry, empathy, and service that she embodies.

ϷϷϷ

# Preface

This book is a celebration of the indomitable spirit and enduring legacy of twenty-one extraordinary individuals from India, whose lives and work have not only shaped the contours of this nation but have also made a profound impact on the world stage. Each story is a testament to the power of determination, vision, and integrity, showcasing how one person's passion and perseverance can indeed change the course of history.

The narratives presented here span a diverse range of fields—from politics and science to arts and sports—reflecting the rich tapestry of India's cultural heritage and its dynamic presence on the global scene. These stories are not just biographies but are inspirational journeys that delve deep into the hearts and minds of individuals who dared to dream big and, more importantly, worked tirelessly to turn their dreams into reality.

India's journey as a nation is intricately woven with the lives of these extraordinary men and women who have faced numerous challenges, overcame staggering obstacles, and emerged victorious, thereby inspiring generations. From the strategic finesse of political leaders who sculpted the modern Indian state to the creative genius of artists and musicians who enchanted both East and West, the characters in this book are as varied as they are fascinating.

The genesis of this book lies in the belief that the stories of these remarkable individuals need to be told and retold, serving as beacons of inspiration for future generations. It seeks to honor their memory and their contributions by presenting their lives not as distant historical narratives but as vibrant and compelling accounts of real-life heroism.

For instance, the tenacity of Mahatma Gandhi, who redefined the power of peaceful protest, or the intellectual prowess of Amartya Sen, whose work in welfare economics has influenced public policy worldwide, are more than just achievements; they are enduring lessons in humility and the power of intellect. Similarly, the courage of Kalpana Chawla, who reached for the stars quite literally and became a global icon for aspiring astronauts, shows that the sky is not the limit when it comes to human aspiration and courage.

This book also highlights the contributions of individuals like Kiran Bedi, whose reforms in the Indian Police Service demonstrate the impact of compassionate leadership in governance. Through her story, we see how empathy and strong ethical convictions can bring about tangible improvements in systems often resistant to change.

In crafting these narratives, I have relied not only on historical data and documented achievements but also on anecdotes and personal accounts that help paint a fuller picture of these personalities. This approach helps bring these icons to life, showing them not just as figures of reverence but as real human beings, complete with flaws and failings, which they transcended in their quest for greatness.

Moreover, this book addresses the profound influence these leaders have had on societal values and cultural shifts within India and how their legacy continues to impact contemporary thought and policy. It aims to contextualize their achievements within the broader narrative of India's development as a society and a nation-state.

As you delve into the pages of this book, you will find yourself on a journey through India's modern history, seen through the lives of its most influential citizens. The stories are designed not only to educate but also to inspire and provoke thought about how each one of us can contribute to society in meaningful ways.

This book is a tribute to the enduring spirit of innovation and resilience that characterizes India and its people. It is hoped that the readers will find in these pages the inspiration to pursue excellence in their own lives and to make a difference to the world around them, just as the twenty-one luminaries discussed here have done. Their lives remind us that with enough determination and grit, it is possible to overcome any obstacle and leave a mark that inspires continents.

*Dr. Minakshi Bansal*
*Social Activist*
*Ahmedabad, Gujarat, Bharat*

❧❧❧

# ONE
# MAHATMA GANDHI

Mahatma Gandhi, born on October 2, 1869, in Porbandar, India, was not only a pivotal figure in the fight for Indian independence but also a beacon of peace and non-violence whose influence transcended national boundaries. His life, filled with profound decisions, resilient karma, and impactful contributions, continues to inspire millions around the globe.

From a young age, Gandhi was imbued with the spirit of seeing beyond the self; his early years were marked by an ordinary upbringing but were steeped in the religious and moral discussions of Jainism, which advocates non-violence towards all living beings. This philosophical grounding was to become the bedrock of his actions and thoughts throughout his life.

Gandhi's journey of transformation began in earnest during his time in South Africa, where he first employed non-violent civil disobedience as a tool for social change. Facing racial discrimination firsthand, Gandhi developed the Satyagraha ('truth-force') philosophy. It was in South Africa that Gandhi made the life-changing decision to renounce the material comforts and adopt a lifestyle of simplicity and self-sufficiency which mirrored his inner quest for truth and justice.

Returning to India in 1915, Gandhi brought with him the refined strategies of passive resistance and was quick to apply them to the Indian context. His leadership in the Champaran and Kheda agitations of 1917 and 1918 marked his emergence as a national figure, showcasing his ability to empathize deeply with the peasantry and effectively mobilize them against unjust laws and practices. These movements were not just campaigns for economic relief, but also for restoring the self-respect and dignity of the oppressed.

Gandhi's decision in 1930 to launch the Salt March, a 240-mile march to the Arabian Sea to produce salt in defiance of British laws, was a masterstroke in symbolic protest. It not only crystallized the struggle against British rule but also galvanized a vast spectrum of Indian society into action. This event underscored his knack for turning ordinary actions into profound symbols of resistance and unity.

Throughout his life, Gandhi's karma was aligned with the principle of 'doing one's duty without attachment to results,' a tenet drawn from the Bhagavad Gita. His commitment to daily routines of prayer, meditation, and community living were reflective of his efforts to live his philosophies rather than merely preach them. His Ashrams were not just residences but living laboratories for experimenting with truth, non-violence, and sustainable living.

Gandhi's positive thoughts were manifested in his unwavering belief in the goodness of human nature and the potential for people to reform. He famously advocated for Hindu-Muslim unity, the upliftment of the downtrodden castes, and the promotion of cottage industries in India, fostering economic independence and social cohesion.

His contributions extended beyond immediate political freedom. Gandhi envisioned an India rooted in rural self-reliance and sustainable living, championing the use of khadi and other village-produced goods to empower the rural economy. His emphasis on education was also transformative, advocating for a curriculum that was hands-on and integrated with life's moral questions.

The impact of Gandhi's life on society is monumental. His philosophy of non-violence inspired movements for civil rights and freedom across the world, influencing leaders such as Martin Luther King Jr. and Nelson Mandela. In India, his teachings continue to be the ethical foundation of many social movements, advocating for a more just and inclusive society.

Gandhi's life was a series of inspirational decisions, a testament to the power of positive action and thought in the face of adversity. His legacy is not just in the freedom India gained under his leadership, but in the ongoing global quest for justice and peace in accordance with the principles of non-violence and truth he so cherished. His message that "be the change you wish to see in the world" remains a timeless call to action, urging individuals to live by the values they espouse.

ppp

*"Mahatma Gandhi taught us that the strength of the soul is invincible, and when harnessed with non-violence, it can shake the very foundations of injustice. Let us remember that true power lies in the serenity of a calm spirit combating turmoil with peaceful resolve."*

ᐅᐅᐅ

# TWO

# DR. APJ ABDUL KALAM

APJ Abdul Kalam, born on October 15, 1931, in the small town of Rameswaram in Tamil Nadu, India, rose from humble beginnings to become a pivotal figure in Indian science and technology, and ultimately served as the nation's 11th President. His journey is not just a tale of personal achievement but a testament to the power of education, vision, and perseverance. Known affectionately as the "Missile Man" for his pioneering work in ballistic missile and launch vehicle technology, Kalam's life was a blend of rich professional achievements and profound personal philosophy.

Kalam's early life was marked by financial struggle, yet enriched by the immeasurable support of his family and educators. Despite these hardships, he excelled in his studies, particularly in physics and aerospace engineering. His academic excellence led him to study at the prestigious Madras Institute of Technology, where his passion for flight and engineering took definitive shape.

His career began at India's Defense Research and Development Organization (DRDO) and later at the Indian Space Research Organization (ISRO), where he was instrumental in propelling India into the small cadre of nations equipped with missile technology.

Kalam's work on the development of the first indigenous Satellite Launch Vehicle (SLV-III) and later missiles like Agni and Prithvi are not just milestones in Indian defense technology but also reflect his belief in self-reliance and indigenous innovation.

The inspirational decisions of Kalam were rooted deeply in his positive vision for his country. One such decision was his instrumental role in the Pokhran-II nuclear tests in 1998, which positioned India as a nuclear state and asserted its standing on the global stage. Despite the international tumult it caused, Kalam saw the tests as crucial for maintaining national security and sovereignty.

Kalam's karma, or actions, were driven by a philosophy of hard work and the relentless pursuit of goals. His dedication was paralleled by a simplicity and integrity that won him the respect of colleagues and adversaries alike. He believed in the power of science and technology to transform society and tirelessly worked towards democratizing these fields, making them accessible to the young minds of India through education and inspirational outreach.

His positive actions extended beyond his professional duties. Kalam was deeply committed to education, believing it to be the primary vehicle for social and economic transformation. He advocated for educational reforms, including curriculum that fostered an innovative spirit and moral uprightness among students. His project 'Providing Urban Amenities to Rural Areas' (PURA), aimed at using technology to bring essential services like water and electricity to India's remote villages, highlights his vision of using scientific knowledge for societal benefits.

Kalam's thoughts were perennially positive, characterized by an unwavering optimism about the potential of youth. He often spoke to students across the country, inspiring them to dream big and nurturing a generation that believes in the power of hard work and vision. His writings, notably his autobiography 'Wings of Fire,' serve as motivational texts for millions.

The contributions of APJ Abdul Kalam are vast and varied. His impact on Indian aerospace and defense technologies is undeniable, but perhaps his most enduring legacy is the cultural shift he inspired towards science and innovation. He made complex scientific concepts accessible and exciting, bringing a sense of adventure to the fields of science and technology.

Kalam's impact on society resonates in the collective mindset of India; he transformed the image of a scientist to one of a national hero and role model. His presidency was marked by approachability and a focus on national development rather than political maneuvering, which endeared him to the hearts of the Indian populace.

His death on July 27, 2015, while delivering a lecture to students, symbolically sealed his commitment to education. The outpouring of grief and respect at his passing from all quarters of society underscored the deep impact of his life and work. Kalam's legacy continues to inspire a new generation of scientists, educators, and thinkers who dream of a better world, driven by the belief in the power of hard work and positive action. His life remains a beacon of the impact that thoughtful, dedicated leadership can have on building a resilient and progressive society.

ᐁᐁᐁ

"APJ Abdul Kalam showed us that dreams
transcend the boundaries of our circumstances,
urging us to reach for the stars while keeping our
feet grounded in hard work and perseverance. His
life reminds us that with passion and dedication,
the sky is not the limit."


ᗧᗧᗧ

# THREE

## SARVEPALLI RADHAKRISHNAN

Sarvepalli Radhakrishnan, born on September 5, 1888, in a small village near Thiruttani, India, emerged as one of the most profound philosophers and statesmen in modern Indian history. Celebrated globally for his intellectual depth and diplomatic acumen, Radhakrishnan's legacy is marked not only by his philosophical teachings but also by his tenure as India's second President. His birthday is celebrated as Teacher's Day in India, reflecting his lifelong dedication to education and his profound respect for teachers.

Raised in a financially constrained but culturally rich Brahmin family, Radhakrishnan was exposed early to religious texts and philosophical discourse, which shaped his intellectual pursuits. Despite financial difficulties, his academic brilliance shone through, earning him scholarships and enabling his education at prestigious institutions including Madras Christian College, where he chose to study philosophy.

Radhakrishnan's academic career was illustrious; he became a professor of philosophy at various colleges, impressing students and peers alike with his insights into Indian philosophy and its relevance to contemporary thought. His interpretation of Indian philosophical texts, particularly the Upanishads and the Bhagavad Gita, as well as his profound understanding of Western philosophy, allowed him to bridge Eastern and Western thought in innovative and enduring ways.

As a philosopher, Radhakrishnan held that philosophy should not be confined to the halls of academia but should be used as a tool to improve everyday life. His approach was practical, focusing on how philosophy could address the challenges of the modern world. This perspective was particularly evident in his first book, "The Philosophy of Rabindranath Tagore," which sought to interpret Tagore's spiritual vision in the context of Indian philosophy and in dialogue with Western traditions.

Radhakrishnan's decisions often reflected his commitment to intellectual and cultural diplomacy. His lectures around the world and his role as an Indian delegate to UNESCO highlighted his belief in the power of educational and cultural exchange to foster global peace and understanding. His tenure as Ambassador to the Soviet Union during the Cold War exemplifies his diplomatic skill and his belief in engagement rather than confrontation.

Appointed as the Vice President and later the President of India, Radhakrishnan was not just a ceremonial figure; he was a moral guide during a period of considerable change and challenge for India. His presidency was marked by grace and the spirit of democratic ideals, reflecting his deep commitment to the principles of justice and equality.

Radhakrishnan's karma, or actions, revolved around his advocacy for a life of virtue and his conviction that education was the most potent tool for social and moral development. He argued consistently for an educational system that was not only rigorous in matters of intellect but also nurturing of ethical and spiritual values.

His positive actions extended to his personal interactions, where he was known for his courtesy, humility, and profound empathy. Stories of his personal kindness and attention to the needs of others, regardless of their social standing, abound, painting a picture of a leader deeply connected to the ethos of service.

Radhakrishnan's contributions to Indian and global thought are vast. His philosophical works continue to be studied for their insight and depth, and his efforts to elevate the status of Indian philosophy on the global stage have had lasting impacts. As an educator, his vision was transformative, advocating for an education system that was deeply rooted in ethical values and broad in its scope, integrating the arts, sciences, and moral philosophy.

The impact of Radhakrishnan on society is both profound and enduring. Celebrating his birthday as Teacher's Day underscores his monumental role in shaping the educational landscape of India, emphasizing the noble profession of teaching and the immense responsibility that educators hold in shaping young minds. His life and work remain a beacon for those in the fields of education, philosophy, and public service, illustrating how intellectual prowess, when combined with moral clarity and civic responsibility, can lead to a life of profound public impact and personal fulfillment.

ᐅᐅᐅ

"Sarvepalli Radhakrishnan's journey from a
scholar to a President illustrates the profound
impact of educators who shape minds with wisdom
and humility. He believed that teachers are the
greatest assets of a society that values knowledge
above all."


ppp

# FOUR

# BAL GANGADHAR TILAK

Bal Gangadhar Tilak, born on July 23, 1856, in Ratnagiri, Maharashtra, was one of the most dynamic leaders of India's struggle for independence. He was famously regarded as one of the prime architects of modern India, with his slogan "Swaraj is my birthright, and I shall have it" becoming the war cry of India's quest for freedom. A staunch advocate of self-rule, Tilak's life and actions were driven by a profound belief in the power of a united Indian populace standing up against British colonial rule.

From his early years, Tilak demonstrated exceptional intelligence and a keen interest in mathematics and Sanskrit. His education at Deccan College in Pune was pivotal, sharpening his analytical skills and deepening his sense of national pride. But more than his academic prowess, it was his political acumen and radical approach towards the freedom movement that marked his contributions to India.

Tilak began his career as a mathematics teacher, but his destiny lay far beyond the confines of a classroom. He quickly turned to journalism and politics, founding two newspapers, 'Kesari' in Marathi and 'The Maratha' in English. These newspapers became vehicles for Tilak's scathing critiques against the colonial government and played a crucial role in awakening the masses to the idea of self-rule.

Tilak's inspirational decisions were characterized by his aggressive stance against British rule. He redefined the Ganapati Festival and the Shivaji Festival, not merely as religious or cultural gatherings but as large-scale public events that stoked the fire of nationalism. This use of cultural symbols and festivals to build a robust sense of community among Indians was a masterstroke in mass mobilization, which later became a cornerstone in India's fight for independence.

His karma or actions, deeply influenced by his ideology, were often controversial yet impactful. Tilak was imprisoned multiple times for his writings and speeches, which the British viewed as seditious. His imprisonment only fueled his resolve and increased his stature among Indians and his global sympathizers. His rigorous imprisonment in Mandalay, Burma, is particularly notable. Despite harsh conditions, he used his time to write the treatise 'Gita Rahasya', a philosophical commentary on the Bhagavad Gita, articulating his vision of active resistance and duty.

Tilak's positive actions were not limited to his direct confrontations with colonial authority. He was instrumental in the establishment of the Deccan Education Society, aiming to improve the quality of education and ensure that education was accessible to all Indians, thus fostering a sense of national pride and self-worth among the youth.

His thoughts were a blend of pragmatism and spirituality. Tilak saw spirituality not as a retreat from the world but as a means of strengthening one's resolve to fight against injustice. He emphasized the ideals of karma yoga, the yoga of action, which he believed was perfectly suited to the needs of the freedom struggle, advocating for righteous action without attachment to the results.

Tilak's contributions extend beyond his role in the independence movement. He also left a significant impact on the Indian legal system, pushing for reforms and the rights of Indians to represent themselves. His legal battles, often fought in the courts where he represented himself, set precedents in Indian jurisprudence.

The impact of Tilak on Indian society was profound. His advocacy of Swaraj laid down the foundational principles for future leaders of the Indian independence movement. His life's work significantly altered the course of Indian history, setting the stage for a nationalistic movement that was based on strong ideals of self-rule and justice.

Bal Gangadhar Tilak's legacy is remembered as one of undying patriotism and relentless pursuit of freedom. His intellectual contributions, particularly in the realms of education, politics, and philosophy, continue to inspire and influence the ethos of India. As a leader, his life was a blend of profound courage, strategic acumen, and a deep-seated love for his country, making him one of the towering figures in the annals of Indian history.

 PPP

"Bal Gangadhar Tilak's unwavering assertion that 'Swaraj is my birthright' ignites the spirit of self-rule and independence within us all. His life encourages us to stand firm in our convictions and fight for our rightful place in the world."

▷▷▷

# FIVE

# SARDAR VALLABHBHAI PATEL

Sardar Vallabhbhai Patel, born on October 31, 1875, in Nadiad, Gujarat, emerged as a stalwart leader in the Indian freedom struggle and played a crucial role in the political integration of India, earning him the title "Iron Man of India." His life is a remarkable narrative of commitment, strategic acumen, and an unwavering dedication to national unity.

Patel's early life did not hint at his future greatness. Born into a farmer's family in a small village, he was largely self-taught in his early years, showing a strong will and determination that would define his later life. His journey into the realms of law began in Godhra and subsequently led him to London, where he trained as a barrister. On returning to India, he established a successful legal practice, but his life took a significant turn when he was introduced to the works and actions of Mahatma Gandhi, which dramatically changed his path.

The pivotal moment in Patel's life came with his overwhelming involvement in the freedom struggle, particularly after witnessing the dire effects of the Jallianwala Bagh massacre in 1919. His organizational skills and determination shone brightly during the

Kheda Satyagraha and the Bardoli Satyagraha, where he led peasants in non-violent civil disobedience against the British-imposed tax regime, earning him the title "Sardar," or leader.

Patel's inspirational decisions are marked by his pragmatic approach to the freedom movement and his stern resolve during the political turbulence following independence. His most monumental task was the integration of over 560 princely states into the Indian Union. His adept diplomacy, stern policies, and sometimes, his willingness to use force when needed, played a decisive role in forging a united India. His ability to negotiate, persuade, and when necessary, push hard, prevented potential balkanization and disintegration at a critical time in India's history.

His karma or actions reflected his deep commitment to unity and integrity. As India's first Home Minister and Deputy Prime Minister, he was instrumental in founding the Indian Administrative Service and the Indian Police Service, structuring them to serve the nation with integrity and effectiveness. His vision extended to the restoration and maintenance of peace and security in the newly independent country, ensuring that the administrative machinery functioned seamlessly amidst the chaotic partition of British India.

Patel's positive thoughts were always geared towards creating a robust, independent, and inclusive India. He believed strongly in the capabilities of Indians to govern themselves and advocated for a balanced approach to governance that included both discipline and compassion. His speeches and writings often emphasized the importance of duty, service, and national pride.

The contributions of Sardar Patel are myriad and deeply embedded in the fabric of modern India. His efforts in integrating the princely states are viewed as nothing short of heroic. Without his intervention, the political landscape of India might have been significantly fragmented, affecting stability and development.

Additionally, his role in developing the civil services created a backbone for the Indian government, ensuring a legacy of administrative competence and governance.

Patel's impact on Indian society is profound. His vision for a united India helped shape the political contours of the newly independent nation. His leadership style, marked by its iron resolve and pragmatism, made him a respected figure among his contemporaries and a revered icon in Indian history. His emphasis on the welfare of farmers and his advocacy for civil rights have left an indelible mark on India's socio-economic policies.

Sardar Vallabhbhai Patel's life and legacy are celebrated annually on his birthday, October 31, declared as Rashtriya Ekta Diwas (National Unity Day). This celebration is a testament to his invaluable contributions to the building of the Indian nation. His strategies, decisions, and the moral force with which he pursued them continue to inspire leaders and citizens alike, embodying the spirit of unity, integrity, and nationalism that is crucial for the sustenance of a vast and diverse country like India. His story remains a beacon of dedication and determination, making him truly the "Iron Man of India."

ᐅᐅᐅ

*"Sardar Vallabhbhai Patel's legacy of unifying India is a testament to the power of determined leadership in the face of division. His vision teaches us that true leadership is found in the courage to build bridges, not barriers."*

❦❦❦

# RAMANUJA

Ramanuja, born in 1017 in the village of Sriperumbudur, Tamil Nadu, is revered as one of the most influential philosophers and theologians in Indian history. His reinterpretation of the Vedanta philosophy and his contributions to the Bhakti movement significantly shaped Hindu thought and religious practice, fostering a more inclusive and devotional approach to spirituality.

From an early age, Ramanuja exhibited an exceptional intellect and a profound interest in spiritual matters. His life took a pivotal turn when he moved to Kanchipuram, where he studied under Yadava Prakasha, a renowned scholar of the Advaita Vedanta school. However, fundamental philosophical disagreements with his teacher led Ramanuja to seek a path that emphasized a more personal and emotional connection with the divine, diverging significantly from the non-dualistic interpretations of his time.

Ramanuja's life was marked by several inspirational decisions that had far-reaching impacts on the religious and social fabric of India. Among the most significant was his commitment to making the esoteric Vedic texts accessible to the common people, breaking centuries of monopoly held by the scholarly classes. He advocated that the path to God did not require renunciation of the world but could be achieved through love and devotion (Bhakti), which anyone could practice regardless of caste or social status.

His karma, or actions, reflected this inclusive vision. Ramanuja traveled extensively across India, visiting major pilgrimage sites and establishing monasteries that became centers of learning. His efforts were not just limited to teaching and writing but also extended to engaging in debates and discussions that helped revive and reform Hindu practices and communities.

One of Ramanuja's most enduring contributions was his philosophical writings, particularly his commentary on the Brahma Sutras—'Sri Bhashya'. In this seminal work, Ramanuja presented the Qualified Non-Dualism (Vishishtadvaita) philosophy, which posits that while the soul and the universe are distinct from Brahman (the ultimate reality), they are also inseparably connected with it, thereby providing a theological basis that supported devotion to a personal god.

Ramanuja's positive thoughts and beliefs were deeply influential in promoting a more devotional path to spirituality. He taught that the ultimate goal of life was to develop an intense love for God, which would culminate in a spiritual union with the divine. His emphasis on devotion (Bhakti) as a means to achieve spiritual liberation introduced a more accessible and emotional dimension to Vedanta philosophy, which resonated with a broad spectrum of society.

Through his actions, Ramanuja left a lasting impact on the Bhakti movement, energizing it with new philosophical foundations and practices that emphasized personal devotion over ritualistic practices. His teachings promoted the idea that devotion to God transcended all barriers of caste and creed, thereby fostering a more inclusive religious environment.

Ramanuja's contributions have had a lasting effect on Indian society, influencing not only religious practices but also social dynamics. His advocacy for equality and his challenge to the caste system encouraged social reform movements within Hinduism that sought to democratize religious practices and make spirituality a matter of personal conviction rather than ritual obligation.

Today, Ramanuja's impact is evident in the rituals and theologies of many Hindu communities, particularly the Sri Vaishnava tradition, which regards him as a saint and a profound teacher. His philosophical writings continue to be studied for their depth and insight, and his life remains a beacon for those who seek to combine deep devotion with rigorous intellectual inquiry.

Ramanuja's legacy as a philosopher, a theologian, and a compassionate leader who sought to bring people closer to the divine through love and devotion is celebrated annually on his birth anniversary. His life and teachings continue to inspire devotion and philosophical inquiry, highlighting his role as a pivotal figure in the revitalization of Indian philosophy and the Bhakti movement.

ppp

"*Ramanuja's philosophy of inclusion in spirituality opens our eyes to the essence of true devotion, which embraces all of humanity without discrimination. His teachings inspire us to see the divine in every soul and the unity in diversity.*"

❧❧❧

# SEVEN

# RABINDRANATH TAGORE

Rabindranath Tagore, born on May 7, 1861, in Kolkata, India, was a polymath whose profound influence as a poet, philosopher, composer, and artist reshaped Bengali literature and music and had a significant impact on the cultural and intellectual landscape of India. Known widely for his poetry and writings, Tagore was also the first non-European to win the Nobel Prize in Literature in 1913, an accolade that celebrated his innovative approach to prose and poetry.

Tagore's upbringing in a family at the forefront of the Bengal Renaissance provided him with a fertile environment for intellectual and artistic growth. His early education was imparted at home under the guidance of tutors; this unconventional schooling helped nurture his creativity and independent thinking. Rejecting formal education, he traveled to England briefly to study law but returned to India without completing his degree to pursue his passion for literature and the arts.

One of Tagore's most inspirational decisions was the establishment of Visva-Bharati University at Santiniketan. His vision for the university was revolutionary—a global center for learning that would break away from the rigid structures of traditional education. At Santiniketan, education was deeply intertwined with nature and the arts, fostering a holistic development of its students. Tagore's approach to education was not merely academic; it emphasized the spiritual and creative growth of the individual, making learning a joyous and life-affirming experience.

Tagore's karma, or actions, were deeply embedded in his philosophy of humanism and his staunch opposition to nationalism and militarism. His criticism of the Raj and his renouncement of his knighthood in protest against the 1919 Jallianwala Bagh massacre in Amritsar, where hundreds of Indians were killed by the British Army, were pivotal moments in his life. These actions highlighted his courage and his commitment to justice and human rights.

His writings and music, through which he expressed his profound thoughts, contributed significantly to shaping the modern Indian identity. As a poet, his most acclaimed work, "Gitanjali," is a collection of poems that meditate on themes such as spirituality and humanity. His lyrical and philosophical depth explored the intersection of the personal with the universal, making his work both accessible and deeply reflective.

Tagore was also the composer of India's national anthem, "Jana Gana Mana," and Bangladesh's national anthem, "Amar Shonar Bangla," which speaks volumes about his impact on national and cultural identity. His music, known as Rabindra Sangeet, is characterized by its blending of classical and folk traditions, and it continues to be integral to the Bengali and broader Indian cultural milieu.

As a social reformer, Tagore's positive thoughts were manifested in his actions and writings. He advocated for the emancipation of women, supported rural development, and promoted an education system that was deeply rooted in one's culture yet open to the streams of knowledge from around the world. He was critical of the caste system and sectarianism, promoting instead a vision of universal brotherhood.

The contributions of Rabindranath Tagore have left an indelible impact on society. His ideas of freedom, education, and national identity continue to inspire and influence not only artistic and literary communities but also movements for social and educational reform in India and around the world. His legacy as a thinker and leader in the arts and his humane vision for society resonate deeply in contemporary times.

In essence, Rabindranath Tagore's life and work encapsulate the integration of the arts, the individual spirit, and the quest for societal progress. His extensive body of work and his philosophical ideologies continue to be celebrated, studied, and admired globally, affirming his role as a beacon of Eastern wisdom and artistic integrity. His philosophical legacy, combined with his humanitarian approach and profound artistic contributions, continues to influence generations, making him a timeless icon of Indian culture.

ppp

"Rabindranath Tagore's poetic genius was not just
in his words, but in his vision of a world where the
mind is without fear and the head is held high. He
reminds us that freedom and knowledge are the
pillars upon which societies thrive."


❦❦❦

# EIGHT

# B.R. AMBEDKAR

B.R. Ambedkar, born on April 14, 1891, in Mhow, India, emerged as a towering figure in the annals of Indian history, revered not only as the principal architect of the Indian Constitution but also as a relentless crusader for social reform. His life's work was dedicated to eradicating social inequality and fighting for the rights of the marginalized, especially Dalits and women, making him one of the most important leaders for social justice in modern India.

Ambedkar's early life was marked by the hardships of caste discrimination, which influenced his lifelong commitment to social justice. Born into a Dalit family, he faced the stigmas and barriers placed by a deeply entrenched caste system. Despite these obstacles, his exceptional intellect and determination led him to pursue higher education—a rarity for Dalits at the time. He earned degrees in economics and political science from Bombay University and later continued his studies abroad at Columbia University and the London School of Economics, where he earned his doctorates.

Returning to India in the 1920s, Ambedkar resolved to fight the injustices faced by the 'untouchables', the term then used for Dalits. His deep understanding of law and justice, coupled with his personal experiences of caste discrimination, fueled his activism and shaped his future endeavors. His decision to use his education for the upliftment of the downtrodden rather than personal gain was one of the first of many inspirational decisions that characterized his career.

Ambedkar's contributions to India are monumental. As an economist, lawyer, and politician, he used his numerous talents to challenge the status quo. His leadership in forming the Bahishkrit Hitakarini Sabha in 1923 marked the beginning of an organized campaign to improve the socio-economic status of Dalits. He also established newspapers like Mooknayak (Leader of the Silent) and Bahishkrit Bharat (Excluded India), which became platforms for advocating Dalit rights.

One of Ambedkar's most significant roles was as the Chairman of the Drafting Committee for the Indian Constitution. In this capacity, he was instrumental in incorporating provisions for safeguarding the rights of minorities and backward classes, ensuring protections that were unprecedented at the time. His advocacy for the principles of liberty, equality, and fraternity is reflected throughout the Indian Constitution.

Ambedkar's karma, or actions, also included advocating for women's rights. He was a key figure in shaping the Hindu Code Bill, which sought to elevate the status of women in terms of inheritance, marriage, and rights within the household. Although the bill faced severe opposition and was not passed in its original form, it laid the groundwork for future reforms.

His positive thoughts were often reflected in his speeches and writings, where he emphasized the importance of education and self-awareness among the oppressed as a means to overcome social barriers. Ambedkar believed that the real remedy for breaking the shackles of the caste system lay in the reform of Hindu religious principles, advocating for a society where social mobility was based on merit rather than birth.

Ambedkar's impact on society is vast. He inspired the Dalit Buddhist movement, encouraging thousands of Dalits to convert to Buddhism as a way to reject the caste system. His leadership continues to inspire numerous political parties, organizations, and movements that champion the cause of social justice.

Ambedkar's legacy is not confined to his role as a legislator or a politician; he was a visionary who envisaged a modern India based on the foundations of justice and equality. His relentless pursuit of social reform has made him a revered figure not only among Dalits but across all sections of Indian society. His writings and speeches continue to be a source of inspiration and a guiding light for policy-making, social reform, and academic discourse in India.

Dr. B.R. Ambedkar's life and work remain a beacon for all those who champion the cause of equality and justice worldwide. As the architect of the Indian Constitution, his profound impact on legal and social reforms has cemented his status as one of the greatest leaders in the history of India's struggle against inequality. His enduring spirit and unwavering commitment to social justice continue to influence the fight for dignity and rights for the marginalized around the globe.

ppp

"B.R. Ambedkar's relentless advocacy for equality
and justice challenges us to confront our prejudices
and strive for a society where everyone has the
opportunity to succeed. His life is a call to dismantle
the barriers of discrimination and build a
foundation of fairness."


ཡཡཡ

# NINE
# MOTHER TERESA

Mother Teresa, born Anjezë Gonxhe Bojaxhiu on August 26, 1910, in Skopje, Macedonia, became one of the most revered figures in the modern world for her selfless charity work and dedication to the care of the sick, poor, and destitute. In 1950, she founded the Missionaries of Charity in Kolkata, India, which grew to become a global beacon of hope and compassion for those in dire need.

From an early age, Mother Teresa was drawn to the lives of missionaries. Her calling to a religious life was clear by the time she was 12, and at 18, she left home to join the Sisters of Loreto in Ireland, never to return to her family home. Her initial years as a nun were spent in Dublin, learning English, before being sent to India, where she began her novitiate in a convent in Darjeeling and was taught the Bengali language and history.

She took her religious vows in 1931, choosing the name Teresa after Saint Thérèse of Lisieux, the patron saint of missionaries. After her vows, she was sent to Calcutta (now Kolkata), where she taught at St. Mary's School for girls. There, she became deeply involved in the lives of the poor, which significantly influenced her subsequent actions and decisions.

Mother Teresa's life took a significant turn on September 10, 1946, during a train journey to Darjeeling, which she described as "the call within the call." She felt a divine urge to leave the convent and help the poor while living among them. This was not a decision made lightly, as it required her to abandon the relative security of the convent and venture into the slums of Calcutta, a city known for its extreme poverty and suffering.

Her inspirational decision to establish the Missionaries of Charity marked a pivotal moment in her life and in the lives of thousands who would be impacted by her work. The organization began as a small group with a simple mission: to care for "the hungry, the naked, the homeless, the crippled, the blind, the lepers, all those people who feel unwanted, unloved, uncared for throughout society, people that have become a burden to the society and are shunned by everyone."

The positive actions of Mother Teresa and her followers can be seen in their extensive charity work, which included the establishment of hospices for those dying of HIV/AIDS, leprosy, and tuberculosis; soup kitchens; dispensaries and mobile clinics; children's and family counseling programs; orphanages; and schools. Her approach was always hands-on, characterized by personal care and a deep sense of dignity for those she served.

Mother Teresa's philosophy was one of uncompromising love and compassion towards all human beings. Her life was a testament to the power of positive thoughts and actions. She believed fervently in the power of love and kindness to change the world, famously saying, "Not all of us can do great things. But we can do small things with great love."

Her contributions to society were internationally recognized when she was awarded the Nobel Peace Prize in 1979. However, her impact extended beyond the awards and accolades. It was felt in the lives of the people she touched, in the smiles of the children she cared for, and in the grateful eyes of the dying whom she comforted in their last moments.

Mother Teresa's influence on society is profound and enduring. Her work inspired countless others to volunteer their services for the needy and the suffering. She created a paradigm for charity that transcends religious and national boundaries—a legacy of unconditional love and service to humanity.

The legacy of Mother Teresa continues to live on through the Missionaries of Charity, which, by her death in 1997, had grown to more than 4,000 sisters, operating 610 missions in over 123 countries. Her life remains a beacon of hope and a reminder of the impact one person can have on the lives of many. Mother Teresa's story is one of faith, compassion, and the unyielding belief in the power of grace to bring light into the darkest corners of human existence.

ppp

*"Mother Teresa's compassionate acts showed that the magnitude of one's influence is measured not by wealth or status, but by the capacity to give love and serve others selflessly. Her example compels us to look beyond ourselves and to care for the forgotten."*

❥❥❥

# TEN

# SWAMI VIVEKANANDA

Swami Vivekananda, born Narendranath Datta on January 12, 1863, in Calcutta, India, emerged as a pivotal figure in the late 19$^{th}$ and early 20$^{th}$ centuries. He played a crucial role in the introduction of the Indian philosophies of Vedanta and Yoga to the Western world and was instrumental in the revival of Hinduism in India. His profound speeches, writings, and his charismatic personality left an indelible mark on the global understanding of Hinduism as a major world religion, reshaping and reforming its perceptions at a time when India was under British rule.

Vivekananda was born into an aristocratic Bengali family of Kolkata. His father was an attorney at the Calcutta High Court, and his mother was a devout housewife. The progressive, rational attitude of his father and the religious temperament of his mother helped shape his thinking and personality. Early in his life, Vivekananda was inclined towards spirituality and had a keen interest in understanding the truth about God and existence.

His intellectual journey at the University of Calcutta was marked by a voracious reading of Western philosophy and history, which he adeptly reconciled with his own understanding of Indian religious and philosophical traditions. The turning point in his life, however, was his meeting with Sri Ramakrishna Paramahansa, a mystic and yogi who would become his guru and spiritual guide. Ramakrishna's teachings on the unity of all religions deeply influenced Vivekananda and shaped his future mission.

One of Vivekananda's most inspirational decisions was to represent India and Hinduism at the Parliament of the World's Religions in Chicago in 1893. His speeches at the Parliament emphasized the importance of tolerance and universal acceptance in fostering peace and human brotherhood. His eloquent advocacy for Hinduism as a religion not just of rituals but as a scientific pursuit of spiritual growth resonated deeply with Western audiences and earned him widespread acclaim.

Vivekananda's karma or actions reflected his deep conviction in the potential of every human being to achieve divine heights through the practice of Yoga and Vedanta. After his success in America, he traveled extensively through Europe, disseminating his guru's teachings and Indian philosophy. His lectures and classes shed light on the philosophical depth of Hinduism and its relevance to the practical aspects of life and spirituality.

His positive actions included the establishment of the Ramakrishna Mission in 1897, which became an institution dedicated to the service of the poor and the needy. The Mission also aimed to propagate the ideals of Vedanta and the holistic development of the human personality as envisaged in Hindu philosophy. Vivekananda's emphasis on service as a means to realize one's own spirituality was a transformative idea that challenged conventional notions of renunciation.

Vivekananda's thoughts and writings continue to inspire and resonate due to their profound philosophical insights and their applicability to personal development and the welfare of society. His call to the youth of India to strive for personal growth as well as the upliftment of the country has motivated countless individuals.

His contributions have had a lasting impact on society. Vivekananda's role in revitalizing Hinduism in India included challenging the caste system and advocating for the upliftment of the downtrodden, positioning Hindu philosophy as a living, evolving, and inclusive tradition. Internationally, his teachings laid the groundwork for the later acceptance of Indian spirituality, yoga, and meditation in the global cultural mainstream.

The legacy of Swami Vivekananda is not merely in his role as a religious and spiritual figure but as a cultural icon who embodied the synthesis of the East and the West. He demonstrated that Indian spirituality could be an important resource for addressing the challenges of modern life and that the wisdom of the Vedas and Upanishads could contribute to the global discourse on spirituality and ethics.

Vivekananda died at the young age of 39 on July 4, 1902, but his teachings and philosophy continue to inspire and shape discussions on spirituality and the role of religion in contemporary society. His vision of a world united by spiritual brotherhood and his belief in the inherent divinity of every individual remain relevant today, making his life and work a beacon for those seeking spiritual enlightenment and social change.

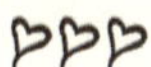

*"Swami Vivekananda's message that each soul is potentially divine motivates us to unlock the vastness of our spirit through service and truth. He taught us that true wisdom comes from understanding the unity of all life."*

ᐅᐅᐅ

# ELEVEN

# LATA MANGESHKAR

Lata Mangeshkar, born on September 28, 1929, in Indore, Madhya Pradesh, India, rose to become one of the most revered and celebrated playback singers in the history of Indian cinema. Often referred to as the "Nightingale of India," her melodious voice and remarkable talent spanned a career of more than seven decades, during which she sang over 30,000 songs in various languages, setting a record that cements her as a monumental figure in the world of music.

Lata's journey into the world of music began in her early childhood, influenced by her father, Pandit Deenanath Mangeshkar, a classical singer and theater actor. Tragedy struck the family when her father passed away in 1942, leaving the young Lata, at just 13 years old, as the main breadwinner for her family. This early responsibility shaped her character, infusing her with a sense of duty and resilience that would mark her entire career.

Her initial foray into singing was not easy. The early years were fraught with challenges, including the struggle to find work and the need to adapt her voice to the demands of film music, which was different from the classical music training she had received. Her big break came in 1949 with the song "Aayega Aanewaala," a haunting melody from the film "Mahal," which catapulted her into the limelight. This song not only showcased her unique vocal ability but also set the stage for a career that would redefine playback singing in India.

Lata's decision to focus on playback singing rather than pursuing a career in classical music was a pivotal one. She brought a new level of professionalism and artistry to playback singing, insisting on the highest standards of music production. Her meticulous attention to detail and her insistence on perfecting every note she sang won her the respect of music directors and her peers.

Throughout her career, Lata's karma or actions were a testament to her dedication to her craft. She worked tirelessly, often recording several songs in a single day, and was known for her disciplined approach to rehearsals and recordings. Her work ethic and professionalism set a standard in the Indian music industry, influencing generations of singers who followed.

Her positive actions extended beyond her professional life. Lata was known for her generosity and her quiet, behind-the-scenes support of many charitable causes. She was particularly known for helping new artists find their footing in the industry, providing them with guidance and opportunities to advance their careers.

Lata's contributions to the arts and culture are vast. She was honored with numerous awards, including the Bharat Ratna, India's highest civilian honor, in 2001, recognizing her extraordinary contributions to Indian music and culture. Her voice became synonymous with the golden age of Indian cinema, and she was the preferred voice for generations of actresses across decades.

Her impact on society extends beyond her music. Lata Mangeshkar was a cultural icon who embodied the spirit of an evolving India. Her songs became anthems for various national causes and sentiments, resonating with the public's aspirations and dreams.

Her rendition of the patriotic song "Ae Mere Watan Ke Logo," which moved Prime Minister Jawaharlal Nehru to tears, is particularly memorable for its emotional impact during a time of national mourning following the India-China war of 1962.

Lata's legacy is multifaceted. As a musician, she pushed the boundaries of what was possible within the realm of playback singing. As a person, her life was a lesson in overcoming adversity with grace and determination. Her enduring popularity and the timeless appeal of her music testify to her profound connection with listeners across generations and geographies.

Lata Mangeshkar's death on February 6, 2022, marked the end of an era in Indian music. However, her songs continue to echo in the hearts of millions, a lasting tribute to a life that was devoted to the pursuit of musical excellence and to touching the lives of others through the power of her voice. Her journey from a child artist struggling to support her family to becoming a legend in Indian music is a profound narrative of resilience, dedication, and the transformative power of art.

ৡৡৡ

"Lata Mangeshkar's melodious voice has not just filled the air with music but has also captured the heart of a nation. Through her songs, she teaches us that art has the power to comfort, unite, and inspire generations."

❧❧❧

# TWELVE

# INDIRA GANDHI

Indira Gandhi, born on November 19, 1917, in Allahabad, India, was a pivotal figure in the political landscape of India, serving as the first and, to date, the only female Prime Minister. Her tenure is remembered for its political ruthlessness and a significant centralization of power, which left a profound impact on the country's governance and its position on the global stage. Her leadership was marked by both significant achievements and controversies, illustrating the complexities of her political and personal life.

Indira was born into the influential Nehru family; her father, Jawaharlal Nehru, was a central figure in Indian politics and the country's first Prime Minister. Growing up in a politically charged environment, she was exposed to the nuances of Indian politics from an early age. Her education at prestigious institutions, including Somerville College, Oxford, provided her with a broad worldview and an understanding of global political trends, which later influenced her political strategies.

Her entry into politics was almost a natural progression, influenced heavily by her family background. Initially working as her father's personal assistant, she gradually moved up the ranks in the Indian National Congress. In 1959, she served as the President of the

Congress Party, which set the stage for her future political career.

One of Indira's most inspirational decisions was the nationalization of banks in 1969. This move was aimed at redistributing wealth and resources more evenly across the burgeoning population of India. It was a bold step that helped to consolidate her power within the party and the country, reflecting her socialist leanings and her commitment to the idea of a self-reliant India. This decision also helped in increasing the reach of banking services in rural areas, contributing to economic inclusivity.

Indira's tenure was also marked by her strong leadership during the Indo-Pakistan War of 1971, which led to the creation of Bangladesh. Her resolve and firm decisions during the war earned her the nickname "Iron Lady" of India. Her foreign policy was characterized by a shift from nonalignment to a more Soviet-friendly policy during the Cold War, which played a crucial role in defining India's international relations during that period.

However, her political career was not without its dark chapters. The most controversial was the declaration of the Emergency in 1975, where civil liberties were curbed, the press was censored, and her political opponents were arrested. The Emergency was a period of significant human rights violations, and it remains a heavily criticized aspect of her legacy. It was during this time that she attempted to implement a forceful campaign of family planning, which also backfired and caused widespread distress among the population.

Despite these controversies, Indira's contributions to India are significant. She was instrumental in the Green Revolution, which transformed India's agricultural landscape, making the country self-sufficient in food grains and significantly reducing famine risks. This initiative has had a lasting impact on India's food security and agricultural productivity.

Indira Gandhi's impact on society and Indian politics was profound. She was a complex figure, driven by a vision of a modern India, yet her methods often sparked debate and dissent. Her assassination on October 31, 1984, by her bodyguards, linked to her actions during Operation Blue Star — the military action against the Golden Temple in Amritsar — was a tragic end to her turbulent career.

Indira Gandhi's legacy is a blend of strength and controversy. Her leadership style and decisions have been studied extensively as they significantly shaped the course of Indian history during the second half of the $20^{th}$ century. Her ability to hold power in a predominantly male-dominated political environment, her vision for India's development, and her complex legacy continue to be of interest to historians, political scientists, and feminists alike.

PPP

"Indira Gandhi's tenure as Prime Minister shows us that leadership involves not just making decisions, but also enduring their gravest consequences. Her legacy is a reminder of the toughness required to steer the ship of a nation."

ᐅᐅᐅ

# THIRTEEN
# C.V. RAMAN

C.V. Raman, born on November 7, 1888, in Tiruchirappalli, Tamil Nadu, stands as one of the most celebrated physicists in history. His groundbreaking work on the scattering of light, which led to the discovery known as the Raman Effect, earned him the Nobel Prize in Physics in 1930. This achievement not only brought him international acclaim but also marked a significant milestone in the development of experimental physics in India.

Raman's early life was characterized by academic excellence. He excelled in his studies at a young age, displaying a remarkable aptitude for science. His intellectual prowess led him to the Presidency College in Madras, where he completed his undergraduate education with top honors. Despite the promising scientific career ahead, Raman initially took up a position in the Indian Finance Department in Calcutta due to financial constraints. However, his passion for science could not be sidelined. He continued his research in physics in the laboratories of the Indian Association for the Cultivation of Science during his spare time, which eventually led to his full-time pursuit of physics.

In 1928, while working as a professor at the University of Calcutta, Raman, along with his student K.S. Krishnan, discovered that when light traverses a transparent material, some of the deflected light changes wavelength and amplitude. This phenomenon, later termed as the Raman Effect, proved to be a powerful argument in favor of the quantum nature of light. The discovery was pivotal not only for its immediate scientific impact but also for its profound implications in the development of quantum mechanics.

Raman's decision to focus on the nature of light scattering was inspired by his deep curiosity about the world around him and a specific interest in why the sea is blue, which he contemplated during a voyage to Europe in 1921. His exploration into the scattering of light led to a deeper understanding of the fundamental properties of light and matter, showcasing his ability to think beyond the conventional scientific paradigms of his time.

His karma or actions were deeply rooted in his commitment to advancing scientific knowledge and education in India. After his Nobel win, he became a national hero and used his stature to promote science among young Indians and to enhance the facilities for scientific research in India. He founded the Raman Research Institute in Bangalore in 1948, where he conducted research until the end of his life.

Raman was not only a scientist but also a visionary thinker and educator. His positive thoughts about the capability of Indian scholars and scientists transformed into concrete actions as he advocated for and built platforms for the future generations of scientists in India. He was instrumental in establishing a culture of research and innovation that has benefitted countless scientists and institutions.

Throughout his career, Raman published extensively, not only on physics but also on the history of science, philosophy, and education. His contributions went beyond the theoretical; they included practical innovations, such as the design and improvement of musical instruments and studies on the optics of minerals and gems.

Despite the accolades and recognition, Raman remained a humble and dedicated scientist, often emphasizing the joy of discovery as his primary reward. His impact on society extends through the many students he inspired, some of whom went on to become distinguished scientists themselves. His work laid the groundwork for Indian scientific research in multiple ways, proving that high-caliber research could be conducted in India.

Raman's legacy is also evident in the continued relevance of his scientific work. The Raman Effect is exploited in various fields, including chemistry, physics, biology, and medicine, particularly in spectroscopic techniques critical in studying molecular structures and dynamics. His life is a testament to the enduring nature of genuine curiosity and relentless pursuit of knowledge.

C.V. Raman passed away on November 21, 1970, but his legacy continues to influence and inspire. As a pioneering scientist and Nobel laureate, his life story is not just a chronicle of scientific achievement but also a narrative of inspiring leadership and enduring impact on the fabric of science and society.

❧❧❧

*"C. V. Raman's discovery of the Raman Effect
unlocks the complex mysteries of light, proving that
perseverance in the face of skepticism can lead to
groundbreaking discoveries. His curiosity reminds
us that questioning the known paths leads to
creating new roads."*

ᐅᐅᐅ

# FOURTEEN
## AMARTYA SEN

Amartya Sen, born on November 3, 1933, in Santiniketan, West Bengal, India, is a distinguished economist and philosopher known for his profound contributions to welfare economics, social choice theory, and economic theories related to poverty, famine, and development. As a recipient of the Nobel Memorial Prize in Economic Sciences in 1998, Sen's innovative approach to economics and ethics has had a profound impact on the formulation of policies aimed at improving human welfare.

Sen's intellectual journey began in the culturally rich environment of Santiniketan, founded by Rabindranath Tagore, which emphasized a broad, humanistic approach to education. This background instilled in him a deep respect for argumentative tradition and heterodoxy, which later became evident in his academic work. He pursued further studies at Presidency College, Kolkata, and then at Trinity College, Cambridge, where he earned his PhD.

The foundation of Sen's influential decisions was laid early in his life when he witnessed the Bengal Famine of 1943. This catastrophic event, which claimed millions of lives, shaped his academic pursuits and his deep concern for the poor and the marginalized. It led him to study economics with a focus on famine, poverty, and welfare, which remained central themes throughout his career.

Sen's most notable contributions to economics include his work on social choice theory, for which he was awarded the Nobel Prize. His development of the capabilities approach redefined the understanding of economic prosperity and poverty. Instead of merely assessing income levels, Sen argued that true welfare depends on what individuals are able to be and do, such as being in good health, having a good job, and being able to participate in society. This framework expanded the view of development to include a range of human capabilities as measures of living standards.

His seminal work, "Poverty and Famines: An Essay on Entitlement and Deprivation" (1981), challenged the conventional view that a lack of food is the most direct cause of famine. Instead, Sen pointed to the lack of access to food — through means such as money, social programs, or job opportunities — as the real issue, thereby shifting the focus from production of food to the distribution of and access to food. This insight had significant policy implications worldwide, influencing approaches to prevent famines and manage food security.

Sen's commitment to the idea of "justice" led him to critique and expand on the philosophical underpinnings of economic theory, particularly in the context of welfare economics. His work emphasized the role of public discussion and democratic participation in the development process, advocating for what he calls "public reasoning" in decision-making.

Sen's positive actions extend beyond his academic contributions. He has been a tireless advocate for gender equality, education, and healthcare, viewing these as fundamental components of development and not merely as outcomes. His advocacy for the expansion of educational and healthcare opportunities in developing countries has influenced many global development policies and initiatives.

In addition to his scholarly work, Sen's influence pervades his teaching and mentoring, having held professorships at prestigious institutions like Harvard, Oxford, and the London School of Economics. Through his pedagogical efforts, Sen has shaped the thinking of generations of economists and philosophers.

Amartya Sen's impact on society can be seen in his influence on the development of human development indices used by the United Nations. His ideas have helped to create more nuanced economic measures that better reflect the complexity of human life. His thoughts and writings have also permeated public debates on welfare, justice, and economics, making him a pivotal figure in both academic and practical policy discussions.

Throughout his career, Sen has demonstrated a commitment to using economic analysis to improve human conditions, blending rigorous scientific methodology with a deep concern for ethical issues. His approach has made him one of the most respected and influential voices in contemporary economics and philosophy.

Sen's extensive body of work and his continuous engagement in public discourse on poverty, freedom, and justice not only reflect his intellectual vigor but also his enduring commitment to human welfare. His legacy is characterized by his ability to transform how we understand and address the most pressing economic and social issues of our time.

ppp

"Amartya Sen's exploration of welfare economics emphasizes that the true measure of a society is found in how it treats its weakest members. His insights challenge us to redefine development as a phenomenon that enriches human lives."

ᐁᐁᐁ

# FIFTEEN

# Ratan Tata

Ratan Tata, born on December 28, 1937, in Bombay, British India, is a prominent Indian industrialist and former chairman of Tata Sons, the principal investment holding company and promoter of Tata companies. Under his stewardship, the Tata Group not only expanded its operations globally but also set new standards in ethical business practices, corporate responsibility, and innovation, significantly shaping the landscape of Indian industry.

Ratan Tata's upbringing in one of India's most influential business families did not shield him from personal challenges. Raised by his grandmother from the age of ten after his parents separated, he grew up with a deep sense of personal responsibility and commitment. His education at the Cathedral and John Connon School in Bombay, followed by Cornell University in the United States where he earned a degree in architecture with structural engineering, and later, the Advanced Management Program at Harvard Business School, equipped him with a broad worldview and a versatile educational background.

Taking over as chairman of Tata Sons in 1991, Ratan Tata faced the daunting task of modernizing and revitalizing a vast but somewhat unwieldy conglomerate. His vision was clear — to streamline operations, focus on innovation, and expand globally. Tata's leadership style, characterized by a quiet but firm determination, was instrumental in transforming the group through a series of bold decisions, including the acquisitions of international brands such as Tetley, Jaguar Land Rover, and Corus, which not only transformed Tata from a largely Indian-centric group into a global business icon but also demonstrated India's capabilities on the international economic stage.

One of Tata's most inspirational decisions was his commitment to ethical business practices and corporate social responsibility. He ensured that the group's expansion and profitability did not come at the cost of ethical standards or societal well-being. This ethos was profoundly illustrated in the development of the Tata Nano, a compact and affordable car designed to provide a safer, more comfortable alternative to the motorcycles used by millions of middle- and lower-income families in India and other developing countries.

Tata's karma, or actions, also reflect his deep humanitarian and social interests. He was personally involved in improving the quality of life for India's underprivileged communities, focusing on areas such as nutrition, education, and rural development, and health care. Under his leadership, Tata companies implemented several programs aimed at empowering communities, improving infrastructure, and fostering sustainable business practices.

Ratan Tata's positive thoughts were often reflected in his humble demeanor and his ability to inspire trust and loyalty among his employees. He believed in leading by example, fostering a culture of innovation, and empowering his team to take risks and think outside the box. This approach not only propelled the Tata Group to new heights but also made it one of the most respected and admired conglomerates globally.

His contributions to industry and society have been widely

recognized with numerous awards and honors, including the Padma Bhushan in 2000 and the Padma Vibhushan in 2008, India's third and second highest civilian awards respectively. He has also been honored with the Carnegie Medal of Philanthropy in 2017 for his efforts to meet the needs of the underprivileged and to foster economic development.

Ratan Tata's impact on society extends far beyond the commercial success of the Tata Group. His visionary leadership in promoting ethical business practices, his commitment to social welfare, and his ability to steer one of India's largest conglomerates through challenging times have made him a role model for business leaders worldwide. His advocacy for corporate accountability and his philanthropic initiatives have set benchmarks for how businesses can contribute to societal development in a meaningful way.

Even after his retirement, Ratan Tata continues to influence various Tata businesses and philanthropic endeavors, demonstrating his ongoing commitment to the group's ethos and his desire to leave a lasting impact on the world. His life and career are not just a testament to his skills as a businessman but also reflect his profound humanity and his unwavering dedication to making a positive difference in the lives of others.

❧❧❧

"Ratan Tata's leadership of the Tata Group exemplifies that the core of true success lies in ethical practices and a commitment to social responsibility. His principles teach us that caring for people and the planet is not just good business—it's the only business that lasts."

ꚜꚜꚜ

# SIXTEEN

# MAHENDRA SINGH DHONI

Mahendra Singh Dhoni, commonly known as M.S. Dhoni, was born on July 7, 1981, in Ranchi, Bihar (now in Jharkhand), India. He rose from modest beginnings to become one of the most celebrated cricketers in the world. Dhoni's illustrious career is marked by his exceptional leadership as the captain of the Indian national cricket team, his strategic acumen, and his cool demeanor under pressure, earning him the nickname "Captain Cool."

Dhoni's journey to international cricket stardom began in his small hometown, where he initially excelled in football and badminton. It was not until his coach pushed him to play cricket that his potential in the sport began to surface. Dhoni worked as a ticket collector for the Indian Railways in his early twenties, a job that he later quit to pursue cricket full-time. His break came with his selection for the national team in 2004, after his performance in the domestic circuit and India A-team caught the selectors' attention.

His rise in international cricket was meteoric. Dhoni quickly established himself as a formidable wicket-keeper and a power-hitter. His ability to finish matches with his calm yet aggressive batting style made him a fan favorite. In 2007, Dhoni was given the captaincy of the Indian T20 team, and under his leadership, India won the inaugural ICC T20 World Cup. His captaincy was characterized by his cool demeanor, sharp strategic mind, and the ability to make bold decisions under pressure.

One of Dhoni's most inspirational decisions came in the 2011 ICC Cricket World Cup final against Sri Lanka. Promoting himself up the batting order in a high-pressure situation, Dhoni played a captain's knock to lead India to its first World Cup victory in 28 years. This decision not only demonstrated his self-belief and leadership qualities but also cemented his status as one of the greatest captains in the history of cricket.

Dhoni's actions on and off the field reflected his karma—his belief in hard work, responsibility, and leading by example. Known for his humility and down-to-earth nature, Dhoni often shied away from the limelight and focused on the team's interests over his own. His tenure as captain is noted for nurturing young talents and for his foresight in building a team that would succeed across all formats of the game.

His positive thoughts and mental strength were evident in how he handled both victories and defeats. Dhoni consistently emphasized the importance of staying balanced and not getting too affected by the outcomes of games. This approach not only made him a great leader but also inspired his teammates to perform their best under pressure.

Dhoni's contributions to Indian cricket are immense. Under his captaincy, India reached the number one ranking in both Test and ODI formats. He is the only captain in the history of cricket to win all three ICC global trophies—the ICC T20 World Cup in 2007, the ICC World Cup in 2011, and the ICC Champions Trophy in 2013. His records and achievements have set high benchmarks for future generations.

Off the field, Dhoni has been involved in various philanthropic activities, including working with children and education programs. His commitment to social causes, coupled with his achievements in cricket, has made him an influential figure in India.

Dhoni's impact on society extends beyond cricket. His life story, from a small-town boy to a sporting legend, is a source of inspiration for many young Indians. He embodies the spirit of perseverance, humility, and the sheer will to succeed against all odds. His biopic, "M.S. Dhoni: The Untold Story," further illustrates his journey and influence, making him a household name across India.

In August 2020, Dhoni announced his retirement from international cricket, leaving behind a legacy characterized by his exceptional leadership, on-field skills, and a new standard for sportsmanship and team spirit. His career remains a testament to the power of determination, strategic thinking, and the profound impact one individual can have on a sport and its nation's psyche.

ᗐᗐᗐ

*"M.S. Dhoni's cool demeanor under pressure illustrates that true strength is staying calm in the storm. His captaincy teaches us that sometimes, silence speaks louder than words and that patience can be the most aggressive strategy."*

▷▷▷

# SEVENTEEN
## KALPANA CHAWLA

Kalpana Chawla, born on March 17, 1962, in Karnal, Haryana, India, became a symbol of courage and inspiration as the first woman of Indian origin in space. Her journey from a small town in India to the vast expanses of space captures the essence of her determined spirit and her relentless pursuit of dreams. Kalpana's life story is not just a narrative of achieving the extraordinary but also serves as a beacon of motivation for countless young women in science and technology.

From a young age, Kalpana was fascinated by the concept of flight. This interest was nurtured by the environment of her hometown, which housed a flying club, and where she would regularly watch planes soar in the sky. Her education began at Tagore Baal Niketan Sr. Secondary School, Karnal, where she excelled in science and mathematics. Her aspirations led her to pursue a degree in Aeronautical Engineering from Punjab Engineering College in Chandigarh, India. Determined to delve deeper into aerospace engineering, she moved to the United States in 1982, where she earned a Master of Science degree in aerospace engineering from the University of Texas at Arlington in 1984. Her academic journey didn't stop there; she went on to complete a second Master's degree in 1986 and a PhD in aerospace engineering in 1988, both from the University of Colorado Boulder.

Kalpana's decision to pursue advanced studies in aerospace engineering in the United States was driven by her ambition to reach the frontiers of space exploration—a field that was, at the time, largely dominated by men and lacked significant representation from Indian women. Her entry into NASA as an astronaut candidate in 1994 marked a significant milestone not only in her career but also in the annals of space history. She was selected for her first space mission in 1996, which culminated in her historic flight aboard the Space Shuttle Columbia in 1997 as a mission specialist and primary robotic arm operator.

The mission was a resounding success and lasted for nearly 16 days as the crew conducted various experiments on microgravity and the environment in space. Kalpana's role was crucial in deploying the Spartan satellite, which studied the outer atmosphere of the sun. Her work during the mission demonstrated her exceptional skills and her ability to contribute significantly to space exploration.

Kalpana's actions and achievements reflect her karma—her belief in hard work, dedication, and her pursuit of excellence. She was known for her meticulous preparation for each mission and her commitment to achieving the objectives set forth by her team. Her positive attitude and her willingness to mentor others exemplified her character and her approach to life and work.

Her second and final space flight on the Space Shuttle Columbia in 2003 ended in tragedy when the spacecraft disintegrated upon re-entry into the Earth's atmosphere, leading to the death of all seven crew members on board. Despite the catastrophic end, Kalpana's legacy continued to inspire and motivate. She became a role model for millions of young girls who aspired to explore the realms of science and technology, showing them that with determination and effort, the sky is not the limit; rather, it's just the beginning.

Kalpana Chawla's contributions to science and space exploration were profound. Her work has had lasting impacts on the study of aerospace and technology, and her life story continues to encourage students, especially girls, to pursue careers in STEM (science, technology, engineering, and mathematics) fields. She broke several barriers and left behind a legacy that transcends national and gender boundaries, making her a global icon of perseverance and strength.

Her impact on society is immeasurable. In her death, she left a poignant message about the risks and sacrifices associated with space exploration but also about the human spirit's boundless capacity to dream and achieve. In memory of her achievements, several scholarships, educational institutions, and awards have been named to honor her contributions and to encourage young minds to follow in her pioneering footsteps.

Kalpana Chawla's life story remains a testament to the power of dreams and the belief that determination, coupled with hard work, can overcome any obstacle. Her journey from the small town of Karnal to the stars is a powerful reminder of human potential and serves as an enduring inspiration to those who dare to dream big.

ᢒᢒᢒ

"Kalpana Chawla's journey into space teaches us that boundaries are meant to be transcended, both in the sky and on the ground. Her legacy inspires us to dream fearlessly and to pursue those dreams relentlessly."

▷▷▷

# EIGHTEEN

# AMITABH BACHCHAN

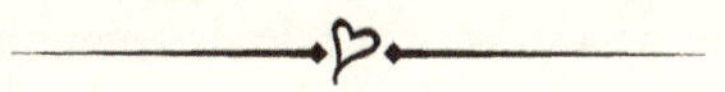

Amitabh Bachchan, born on October 11, 1942, in Allahabad, India, to Hindi poet Harivansh Rai Bachchan and social activist Teji Bachchan, has been a towering figure in the world of Indian cinema for over five decades. His journey from a young man struggling to find his voice in the movie industry to becoming an icon of Indian cinema is a narrative of resilience, reinvention, and enduring charm. Bachchan's career, characterized by its depth and diversity, has made him one of the most influential and respected actors in the history of film.

Bachchan's early years were marked by a rigorous education and a deep immersion in the arts, influenced by his father's literary work. He attended Sherwood College in Nainital and later Delhi University. Despite a promising job as a freight broker for the shipping firm, Bird and Co., Bachchan was drawn to the allure of acting. In 1969, he made his film debut in "Saat Hindustani." Despite its modest success, the film marked the beginning of a career that would set new standards in Indian cinema.

Amitabh Bachchan's rise to stardom was not immediate. His early years in the industry were challenging, with a string of unsuccessful films. However, his fortune changed dramatically in 1973 with the film "Zanjeer," in which he played the iconic role of Inspector Vijay Khanna. The character, marked by its brooding intensity, redefined the Hindi film hero and positioned Bachchan as the "angry young man" of Bollywood. This role resonated deeply with the audience at a time when India was grappling with social and economic upheavals, making him a voice for the disenfranchised.

Bachchan's career in the 1970s and 1980s is an anthology of seminal films that span genres and showcase his versatility as an actor. Films like "Deewaar," "Sholay," and "Amar Akbar Anthony" not only cemented his status as a superstar but also demonstrated his ability to deliver powerful performances that captured the imagination of the Indian public. His commanding screen presence, deep baritone voice, and dynamic acting style made him an icon for multiple generations.

The 1982 accident on the set of "Coolie" marked a significant turn in Bachchan's life and career. He suffered a near-fatal injury during a fight scene, which led to a nationwide outpouring of support for him, underscoring his deep connection with the Indian populace. His recovery and subsequent return to the big screen were seen as symbolic of his fighting spirit, further endearing him to the hearts of his fans.

In the late 1990s, after a brief stint in politics and a series of commercial failures, Bachchan faced financial adversity with his entertainment company, ABCL. However, his career witnessed a remarkable resurgence with his return as the host of the television game show "Kaun Banega Crorepati" in 2000. The show not only brought him back into the limelight but also redefined celebrity involvement in Indian television.

Bachchan's karma or actions reflect a blend of professional dedication and a commitment to social causes. He has been involved in numerous charitable endeavors, supporting causes related to health, education, and disaster relief. His decision to pay off the debts of several farmers and to support the families of Indian soldiers reflects his compassionate approach to his stature and influence.

Throughout his career, Bachchan has been a recipient of numerous awards, including the Padma Shri, the Padma Bhushan, and the Padma Vibhushan, reflecting his contributions to the arts and Indian society at large. His roles in recent films continue to garner critical acclaim, proving his enduring appeal and versatility as an actor.

Amitabh Bachchan's impact on Indian cinema and society is profound. His journey from a voice of the turbulent times of the 1970s to a celebrated elder statesman of Indian cinema is a testament to his enduring talent and adaptability. His life and career continue to inspire aspiring actors and filmmakers, embodying the spirit of perseverance and transformation that characterizes the best of cinematic and personal legacies.

ppp

"Amitabh Bachchan's enduring career in cinema shows that reinvention is the key to longevity. His journey teaches us that in every role life gives us, there is an opportunity to create something memorable."

❦❦❦

# NINETEEN

# VISWANATHAN ANAND

Viswanathan Anand, born on December 11, 1969, in Chennai, Tamil Nadu, India, is a pioneering figure in the world of chess, renowned not only as one of the greatest chess players of all time but also as a former World Chess Champion who played a crucial role in popularizing chess in India. Known for his rapid playing speed and intuitive style, Anand's achievements have made him a national hero and an inspiration to countless aspiring chess players across the globe.

Anand's interest in chess began at an early age, largely influenced by his mother, who introduced him to the game when he was six years old. His natural talent for chess was evident from the beginning, as he quickly grasped complex strategies and tactics. By the age of fourteen, Anand had won the National Sub-Junior Chess Championship, marking the start of a glittering career that would see him reach the pinnacle of the chess world.

Anand's journey on the international chess circuit began with his participation in the World Junior Chess Championship in 1983. His victory in this championship in 1987 was India's first in the category and served as a prelude to his illustrious career. He earned the title of International Master at the age of fifteen and became India's first Grandmaster at the age of eighteen, breaking many age records along the way.

One of Anand's most inspirational decisions came in the mid-1990s when he decided to shift his base to Spain to compete more effectively at the highest levels of chess. This move was strategic, allowing him better access to top-tier tournaments and training opportunities in Europe, where chess was more vigorously competitive. His dedication and willingness to adapt were key factors that helped him stay at the top of the game for decades.

In 2000, Anand achieved a significant milestone by winning the FIDE World Chess Championship, thus becoming India's first official World Champion. This victory was not just a personal achievement but a monumental moment for Indian chess, inspiring a new generation of players. Anand's continued success on the global stage, including winning the World Chess Championship in 2007, 2008, 2010, and 2012, established him as one of the elite players in the chess world.

Anand's positive actions extend beyond his achievements on the chessboard. He has been actively involved in promoting chess as an educational tool in India, encouraging children to take up the game to improve cognitive skills and learning abilities. His involvement in chess education programs has helped spread the game across different socio-economic segments in India, making it accessible to a broader audience.

Anand's contributions to society through chess are profound. He has served as a role model for sportsmanship and intellectual competitiveness, showing that it is possible to be a fierce competitor while maintaining dignity and respect for opponents. His approachable demeanor and willingness to engage with fans have made him a beloved figure.

Moreover, Anand has utilized his fame and resources to support various charitable causes, particularly those related to children and education. He has been part of numerous campaigns focused on raising awareness about the benefits of chess for young minds, including improving problem-solving skills, enhancing memory, and fostering a strategic thinking process.

Throughout his career, Anand has been the recipient of numerous awards, including the Padma Shri, the Padma Bhushan, and the Padma Vibhushan, India's fourth, third, and second highest civilian awards, respectively. These honors reflect not only his achievements in the realm of chess but also his impact on Indian sports and culture.

Viswanathan Anand's legacy in chess and his impact on society underscore his pivotal role in transforming chess from a niche pursuit into a mainstream sport in India. His life story is a testament to the power of dedication, strategic thinking, and passion, inspiring not only aspiring chess players but all individuals striving for excellence in their respective fields. His career continues to inspire and shape the future of chess, both in India and around the world, ensuring that his influence will be felt for generations to come.

ᐅᐅᐅ

*"Viswanathan Anand's mastery over chess reveals that every move we make can change the course of our life's game. His strategic thinking encourages us to always be two steps ahead in our actions and thoughts."*

ᗡᗡᗡ

# TWENTY

# J.R.D. TATA

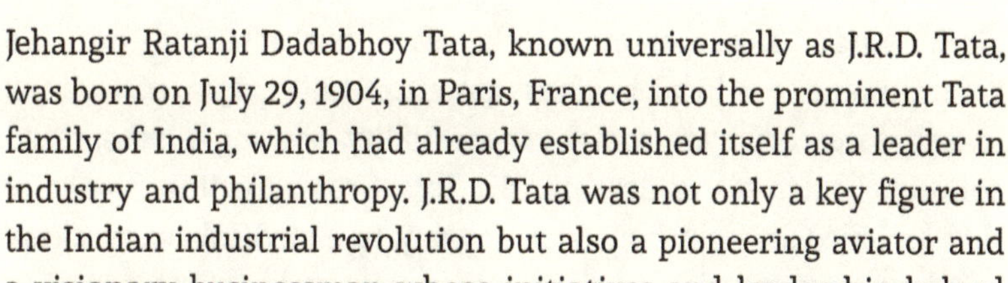

Jehangir Ratanji Dadabhoy Tata, known universally as J.R.D. Tata, was born on July 29, 1904, in Paris, France, into the prominent Tata family of India, which had already established itself as a leader in industry and philanthropy. J.R.D. Tata was not only a key figure in the Indian industrial revolution but also a pioneering aviator and a visionary businessman whose initiatives and leadership helped transform the Tata Group into a conglomerate of global significance.

From an early age, J.R.D. was exposed to a diverse cultural environment, owing to his French mother and Indian father. He was educated in France, Japan, and England, and later attended the Cathedral and John Connon School in Bombay (now Mumbai), India. At the age of 15, he was sent to France to train as an engineer but soon discovered his passion for flying, which would shape much of his later career.

J.R.D. Tata's journey in business began when he joined the Tata Company in 1925, and by 1938, at the age of 34, he was appointed as the Chairman of Tata Sons, making him the youngest head of the largest industrial group in India. Under his stewardship, the Tata Group expanded rapidly, founding over a hundred companies, including major ventures like Tata Motors, Tata Consultancy

Services, and Titan Industries.

One of J.R.D.'s most significant contributions was in the field of aviation. He founded India's first commercial airline, Tata Airlines, in 1932, which later became Air India in 1946. His pioneering efforts in this field earned him the distinction of being India's first licensed pilot. J.R.D.'s vision for aviation in India was clear — he believed that air travel would be crucial to the country's development and connectivity. His dedication culminated in Air India becoming one of the most prestigious airlines globally, known for its high standards of service and safety.

J.R.D. Tata's management style was characterized by his commitment to ethical business practices and employee welfare, long before corporate social responsibility became a recognized concept. Under his leadership, the Tata Group instituted policies that included an eight-hour working day, free medical aid, workers' accident compensation schemes, and maternity benefits for women — all of which were revolutionary at the time.

His karma, or actions, also reflected his belief in the importance of giving back to society. J.R.D. was instrumental in establishing several institutions of national importance in India, including the Tata Institute of Social Sciences, the Tata Institute of Fundamental Research, and the National Centre for the Performing Arts. His commitment to improving the quality of life in India was not limited to business; he also played a key role in the establishment of the city of Jamshedpur, where Tata Steel is located, planning it as a model town with excellent housing, sanitation, and education facilities.

J.R.D. Tata was also a forward-thinking environmentalist, emphasizing sustainable practices and the importance of preserving the natural environment long before environmental conservation became mainstream. His vision and practices have left a lasting legacy within the Tata Group, with ongoing commitments to sustainability.

J.R.D.'s influence extended beyond business and industry. He was a proponent of family planning, women's rights, and a more egalitarian society. His positive thoughts and inclusive approach to business and society helped shape modern Indian industrial policies and practices, influencing generations of entrepreneurs and business leaders.

For his contributions to Indian industry and society, J.R.D. Tata was conferred with many awards and honors, including the Bharat Ratna, India's highest civilian award, in 1992. His legacy is not merely that of a successful businessman but of a visionary who helped to mold the industrial landscape of India.

J.R.D. Tata passed away on November 29, 1993, but his ideals and visions continue to guide the Tata Group and serve as a beacon for responsible leadership and ethical business practices around the world. His life remains a testament to the power of innovative thinking, ethical leadership, and committed philanthropy, inspiring future generations to aspire not just to achieve professional success but to contribute meaningfully to society at large.

ppp

*"J.R.D. Tata's vision for India's industrial future was built on the bedrock of sustainability and ethical entrepreneurship. His life reminds us that real progress respects both people and the environment."*

▷▷▷

# TWENTY-ONE
## KIRAN BEDI

Kiran Bedi, born on June 9, 1949, in Amritsar, Punjab, India, stands out as a trailblazer and an exemplary figure in Indian law enforcement and social reform. She carved a niche for herself in a male-dominated profession as the first woman to join the Indian Police Service (IPS) in 1972. Throughout her career, Bedi not only broke glass ceilings but also redefined the parameters of police service through her innovative and humane approaches to law enforcement and prison reform.

Raised in a family that valued education and empowerment, Kiran was encouraged to pursue her ambitions unabated by traditional gender roles. She excelled academically and was also a tennis champion, participating in national and international tournaments. Bedi's educational journey in political science culminated in a doctoral degree on the topic of drug abuse and domestic violence, equipping her with an understanding of the social issues that she would later tackle professionally.

Joining the IPS was a defiant decision against the normative expectations of society regarding women's roles and careers at the time. Her entry into the IPS marked the beginning of a series of pioneering efforts aimed at transforming Indian policing. Kiran Bedi's first major assignment was as the Assistant Superintendent of Police in Chanakyapuri, Delhi, where she demonstrated her commitment to upholding the law with strictness combined with sensitivity.

Perhaps the most transformative period of her career came when she was appointed the Inspector General of Tihar Jail in 1993. At that time, Tihar Jail was notorious for its harsh conditions and the inhumane treatment of prisoners. Bedi's approach to prison management was revolutionary. She initiated a number of reforms aimed at transforming the prison into a rehabilitative institution rather than merely a punitive facility. She introduced various educational and vocational training programs for inmates, launched yoga and meditation classes, and established a full-fledged open university within the jail premises. Her program, named 'Navjyoti,' significantly improved the prison environment and became a model for prison reforms globally.

Kiran Bedi's belief in restorative justice—rehabilitating offenders through reconciliation with victims and the community at large—reshaped conventional practices. Her initiatives such as organizing 'Darbars' - a forum where prisoners could voice their concerns directly to the authorities - were part of her efforts to humanize the treatment of the incarcerated. Her focus was not just on punishment but on recovery and preparation for reintegration into society.

Throughout her service in the police force, Bedi was known for her integrity and courage. Her no-nonsense approach to corruption and her efforts to make the police force more accessible and responsive to the public earned her the nickname "Crane Bedi" after she towed the Prime Minister's car for a parking violation. This incident epitomized her commitment to the rule of law, demonstrating that no one was above it, thereby fostering a culture of accountability.

After her retirement in 2007, Kiran Bedi turned her focus to social activism and education, founding two NGOs that work in the fields of police reform, prison reform, women's rights, and rural and community development. Her efforts have continued to emphasize the importance of education, governance, and community participation.

Kiran Bedi's contributions have been widely recognized. She has been the recipient of numerous awards, including the Ramon Magsaysay Award (also called the Asian Nobel Prize) in 1994 for Government Service.

Her life's work has had a profound impact on Indian society, particularly in terms of improving the interactions between the police and the community and enhancing the focus on reformative rather than merely punitive justice. Her career is a testament to the power of strong leadership, vision, and relentless perseverance in the face of challenges.

Kiran Bedi's journey from a trailblazing police officer to a social activist and educator is not just a personal achievement but a monumental contribution to societal progress. She continues to inspire countless young women and men to public service, making her story a beacon of hope and a case study in impactful leadership.

ppp

"Kiran Bedi's reformative work in the Indian Police
Service exemplifies that change requires courage
and compassion in equal measure. Her legacy urges
us to enforce the law not just with our might, but
with our heart as well.

ᐳᐳᐳ

# TWENTY-TWO

# MAHAMANA PANDIT MADAN MOHAN MALVIYA

Mahamana Pandit Madan Mohan Malviya, born on December 25, 1861, in Allahabad, was a distinguished Indian educationist, lawyer, and freedom fighter, best known for founding the Banaras Hindu University (BHU) in Varanasi, one of the largest residential universities in Asia. His life is a testament to his dedication to education and his profound influence on the nationalist movement in India.

Malviya's early life was marked by a deep-rooted affinity for education and learning. Raised in a family that valued literature and activism, he was influenced by his father, Pandit Brij Nath, a learned man himself. Malviya completed his education from Muir Central College, later known as Allahabad University, where he studied Sanskrit, English literature, and Indian history, which stoked his interests in Indian culture and education.

Starting his career as a schoolteacher and later, as an editor of English and Hindi editions of the "Indian Opinion," Malviya's early professional life was dedicated to journalism and writing. His articles and writings often focused on public welfare and vehemently criticized the policies of the ruling British government, showcasing his early nationalist sentiments.

In 1887, Malviya qualified as a lawyer and soon gained prominence in Allahabad High Court. However, his legal practice was always interspersed with his commitment to public service and educational pursuits. His decision to enter politics was driven by a desire to effect more substantive changes; he served four terms as president of the Indian National Congress starting in 1909. His tenure in politics was marked by efforts to promote Hindu-Muslim unity, a testament to his vision of a cohesive and united India.

Perhaps the most significant decision of Malviya's career was the founding of the Banaras Hindu University in 1916. He envisioned BHU as a center of learning that would combine the best of Eastern and Western curricula and promote the study of Hindu culture, religion, and philosophy alongside contemporary subjects from the sciences and the humanities. This initiative was revolutionary, coming at a time when India's education system was overwhelmingly influenced by British models and policies.

Malviya's fundraising campaigns for BHU were a monumental feat, involving extensive travels across India to gain support from princes, businessmen, and common folk alike. His efforts culminated in the successful establishment of the university, which became a hub for intellectual activity and nationalism. BHU has produced many distinguished scholars and contributes immensely to the cultural and scientific development of India.

In his later years, Malviya was also a staunch advocate of civil rights and an opponent of untouchability. He supported Gandhi's calls for civil disobedience and was an active participant in the non-cooperation movement, for which he was arrested in 1932.

Throughout his life, his advocacy for Hindu values was complemented by a commitment to inclusivity and social reform.

Malviya's karma or actions were deeply rooted in his positive thoughts about the role of education in uplifting society. He believed in the power of knowledge and education to drive social change and was often quoted as saying that a library was a more potent weapon than a battle-axe. Under his leadership, BHU set up several colleges, including medical and engineering institutions, during his lifetime, contributing significantly to the education sector in India.

Pandit Madan Mohan Malviya's legacy is multifaceted. As a freedom fighter, his contribution to India's independence movement was significant. As an educationist, his legacy is carried forward by Banaras Hindu University, a testament to his vision for an independent system of education that was deeply Indian at its core yet open to the progressive aspects of Western academia.

He was posthumously awarded the Bharat Ratna, India's highest civilian award, in 2014, an acknowledgment of his enduring contributions to the nation in education and public life. Malviya's life continues to inspire educationalists and leaders around the country, serving as a beacon of virtue, perseverance, and dedication to the public good. His deep humanity and visionary educational practices remain relevant, reminding us of the transformative power of education and civic responsibility.

ᗑᗑᗑ

"Mahamana Pandit Madan Mohan Malviya's
commitment to education as the bedrock of society
illustrates his profound belief in the power of
learning to elevate the human spirit. He founded
Banaras Hindu University with the vision that
knowledge should be accessible to all, regardless of
background, fostering a community where every
student could thrive. His life teaches us that true
wisdom lies in building institutions that outlast us,
serving generations to come with the light of
enlightenment."

▷▷▷

# TWENTY-THREE
## SUMMARY

This chapter provides a synthesized overview of the lives and contributions of twenty-two distinguished individuals from diverse fields. Each figure exemplifies unique traits and achievements that have significantly impacted society, culture, and their respective disciplines. Through an exploration of their journeys, decisions, and enduring legacies, this summary aims to encapsulate their contributions to Indian and global heritage.

**1. Mahatma Gandhi:** Known as the father of the Indian nation, Gandhi's philosophy of non-violence and truth led India to independence. His methods of civil disobedience influenced worldwide movements for civil rights and freedom.

**2. APJ Abdul Kalam:** India's 11th president and a pioneering aerospace scientist, Kalam's role in India's missile development program earned him the title "Missile Man." His presidency and writings inspired millions of young people to dream big and pursue their passions.

**3. Sarvepalli Radhakrishnan:** Esteemed philosopher and India's second president, Radhakrishnan promoted Indian philosophy on a global stage, redefining the link between philosophy and practical life, and was instrumental in shaping contemporary Hindu identity.

**4. Bal Gangadhar Tilak:** Known for his quote "Swaraj is my birthright," Tilak was a prominent freedom fighter whose advocacy of swaraj or self-rule was a significant step towards India gaining independence.

**5. Sardar Vallabhbhai Patel:** A key figure in India's struggle for independence and the political integration of India, Patel's efforts in uniting the nation earned him the title "Iron Man of India."

**6. Ramanuja:** Influential philosopher and theologian, Ramanuja's contributions to the Indian philosophy of Vedanta and the Bhakti movement significantly advanced Hindu theology and philosophy.

**7. Rabindranath Tagore:** Nobel laureate Tagore reshaped Bengali literature, music, and Indian art in the late 19th and early 20th centuries. His visionary works and ideas continue to influence art and culture worldwide.

**8. B.R. Ambedkar:** Architect of the Indian Constitution and a fervent advocate for social reform, especially concerning Dalits and women. Ambedkar's legal acumen and commitment to equality shaped modern India's legal and social landscape.

**9. Mother Teresa:** Nobel Peace Prize-winning missionary known for her charity work in Kolkata, Mother Teresa's profound compassion and dedication to the destitute and sick made her an icon of selfless service.

**10. Swami Vivekananda:** His teachings on Vedanta and Yoga in the late 19th century introduced the West to Indian philosophies. Vivekananda's emphasis on spirituality and values inspired an ethical and philosophical awakening.

**11. Lata Mangeshkar:** Renowned as the "Nightingale of India,"

Mangeshkar's voice defined much of Indian cinema's musical history. Her career, spanning over seven decades, left a lasting legacy in the world of music.

**12. Indira Gandhi:** As India's first and only female prime minister to date, Gandhi was a dynamic leader whose policies and actions significantly shaped the 20th-century political landscape of India.

**13. C.V. Raman:** Nobel laureate in Physics, Raman's discovery of the Raman Effect contributed significantly to the field of quantum physics, enhancing our understanding of molecular energy and light scattering.

**14. Amartya Sen:** His contributions to welfare economics and social choice theory made him a pivotal figure in contemporary economic thought, advocating for policies that emphasize human well-being and economic justice.

**15. Ratan Tata:** Under his leadership, the Tata Group expanded globally, and he was instrumental in founding numerous enterprises, including Tata Motors and Tata Consultancy Services, which propelled Indian industry onto the world stage.

**16. M.S. Dhoni:** Renowned cricketer and former captain of the Indian national team, Dhoni is celebrated for his cool demeanor and sharp leadership, which brought numerous victories and accolades to Indian cricket.

**17. Kalpana Chawla:** The first woman of Indian origin in space, Chawla was a role model for women in science and technology. Her tragic death in the Columbia space shuttle disaster marked her as a brave pioneer of space exploration.

**18. Amitabh Bachchan:** A legendary figure in Indian cinema, Bachchan's career spans over five decades during which he became one of the most influential actors in the history of Indian films.

**19. Viswanathan Anand:** A former World Chess Champion, Anand popularized chess in India, bringing it to the masses and achieving unprecedented success in international chess.

**20. J.R.D. Tata:** As a pioneering aviator and a key businessman, J.R.D. Tata founded several industries under the Tata Group. His visionary leadership and commitment to ethical business practices significantly influenced Indian industry.

**21. Kiran Bedi:** The first woman to join the Indian Police Service, Bedi's reformative focus on humane treatment of prisoners and advocacy for police and prison reform have made her a key figure in Indian law enforcement and social justice.

ÞÞÞ

# Citation And References

*This book represents the culmination of extensive research and meticulous analysis, incorporating a diverse range of sources, including numerous books, scholarly studies, and personal experiences. Additionally, I have scoured various websites to gather relevant information and data essential for the compilation of this work. I have taken every precaution to ensure the accuracy of the information presented and have diligently cited all sources to acknowledge their contributions.*

*Despite these efforts, the possibility of inadvertent errors remains. I deeply value the insights of my readers and appreciate any feedback that can help identify and rectify such inaccuracies. I encourage you to bring any discrepancies to my attention.*

*Your feedback is not only welcome but crucial, as it will aid in correcting current editions and enhancing the content of future ones. I am committed to maintaining the highest standards of accuracy and reliability in my work and thank you for your support and understanding.*

*Additionally, I firmly uphold the principle of freedom of speech and expression as guaranteed under Article 19(1)(a) of the Constitution of India, and I respect the diverse viewpoints and expressions of all readers.*

ᐅᐅᐅ

# Other Books Of The Author

1. Empowering Minds: A Journey into Women's Self-Discovery and Power
2. The Dynamics of Motivation: Catalyzing Thought into Action
3. Meditation and Mental Well Being: The Path to Inner Peace and Clarity
4. The Psychology of Child Education: Nurturing Future Generations
5. Ethical Enlightenment: A Modern Guide to Living with Integrity
6. Voices of Empowerment: Stories of Women Rising Against Odds
7. Social Psychology in Everyday Life: Understanding Human Connections
8. The Essence of Motivational Speaking: Inspiring Change in Others
9. Balancing Acts: Women, Work, and the Will to Lead
10. Guiding with Grace: Raising Children with Compassion and Awareness
11. The Power of Positive Aging: Embracing Life After Fifty
12. Building Resilient Communities: Social Work in Action
13. The Ethical Educator: Principles for Teaching and Learning
14. From Insight to Impact: Social Psychology for a Better World
15. The Ethics of Empathy: A Guide to Ethical Living
16. The Science of Empowering the Self: Navigating Life's Challenges with Psychological Wisdom
17. The Mindful Conscious Leader: Meditation Techniques for Modern Management
18. Pioneering Spirit: Women's Pathways to Leadership and Empowerment
19. Feeling to Healing: The Role of Emotional Intelligence in Child Development
20. Transformative Talks and Words of Inspiration: Insights into Motivational Oratory

ÞÞÞ

# Contact


Dr. Minakshi Bansal
Social Activist
Ahmedabad, Gujarat, Bharat
minakshiindiag20@yahoo.com


≻≻≻

|| LOKAHA SAMASTHAHA SUKHINO BHAVANTU ||